Do I Belong? offers a faith-based understanding of adoption, both as a picture of God's love and as a way to grow one's family. As adoptive parents ourselves, we know there are challenges that accompany the joys; this book addresses those challenges with sound biblical ideas to apply during and after the adoption process.

SAM AND MARY BROWNBACK, former Kansas governor and first lady

As someone who spent time in the foster care system, I have a heart for kids who are awaiting their "forever family." Even after that dream comes true, however, many questions and emotions remain. In this encouraging book for kids, Carey Koenig and two of her adopted children, Reid and Halley, take an honest look at the joys and challenges of adoption—and offer words of hope. *Do I Belong?* helps kids adopted from foster care learn to embrace their identity as a beloved child of their parents and a precious son or daughter of their heavenly Father.

JIM DALY, president and CEO of Focus on the Family

Carey, Reid, and Halley Koenig have filled a critical need for adoptive families. Written in an age-appropriate, easy-to-read format that's sure to spark thoughtful discussions, *Do I Belong?* captures the issues that kids who were adopted face today. As a foster parent to twenty-three children and biological mother to five, I wish this book had been on my family's bookshelf a long time ago. Any family involved with adoption will be blessed by the Koenigs' thoughtful perspective.

MICHELE BACHMANN, former United States representative from Minnesota

Do I Belong? is written for children and youth who, like all mankind, hunger for peace through being connected to family. This book is a reminder that even when we have questions, the answer remains that we all belong to the Father.

DR. SHAREN FORD, director of foster care and adoption for Focus on the Family

When we adopt children from foster care, we know some of the questions our children have because they ask them out loud. But there are other questions we may know nothing about. And even if we did, would we know how to answer them? *Do I Belong?* provides a great starting point for important conversations that can lead to connection with your children and help them feel seen.

JASON WEBER, author, speaker, and national director of More Than Enough at the Christian Alliance for Orphans

As a child adopted from the foster care system, I wish there would have been a resource like this for my parents to share with me. What makes this book special is the way the authors integrate feelings, thoughts, questions, and Scripture together in such a conversational way.

BOB J. BRUDER-MATTSON, president and CEO of FaithBridge Foster Care

Do I Belong?

Do I Belong?

Reassuring Kids Adopted from Foster Care

CAREY KOENIG, REID KOENIG & HALLEY KOENIG

FOCUS
ON THE FAMILY.

A Focus on the Family resource
published by Tyndale House Publishers

Contents

DO I BELONG?

THERE ARE MORE THAN FOUR HUNDRED THOUSAND CHILDREN IN FOSTER CARE TODAY,

and you were once one of those kids. For whatever reason, your birth parents or guardians were unable to care for you, even though they love you. Children like you are sometimes removed from their homes so that these caregivers can receive help and so that you can be safe and taken care of the way you deserve to be. Many caregivers do get the help they need, and the children are able to return to their families. But other times the kids remain in the foster care system until they are adopted into a forever family.

Now that you're out of the foster care system and have been adopted, your life is different, right? You and your family love each other, but you might also disagree sometimes. Some days are good, and some days are rough.

Depending on your situation and how old you were when you were adopted, you might still have some bad memories from the past. And those experiences might still affect you. You probably have questions and even confused feelings about your birth family, your time in foster care, and even your family now.

Having questions about these things isn't wrong. Not at all. Whether you've been a part of your forever family for a few weeks or several years, it's completely natural to sometimes wonder: *Do I belong?*

This book is based on our experiences building a family through adoption and looking for answers to our questions. We want to share with others what we've learned. We talked to some pretty smart grown-ups who have studied adoption and foster care for a long time. We also talked to different kids just like you who were adopted from foster care. We wanted to hear about what they went through and the questions they have. We'll answer several of those questions in this book. We've also included questions at the end of each chapter that you can talk about with your parents. Or you can write down your answers in a journal.

In the pages that follow, you'll hear from kids like John. He knows that God has a plan for all that happened to him; he's just not sure what that plan is yet. He wants to know why God created adoption in the first place.

You'll meet Abby, who spent time with multiple foster families. Some said they were going to adopt her but never did. Finally, one of her foster families kept their word and adopted her, but it felt unfair that she'd had to live in so many places. Is it okay that she still gets mad sometimes?

You'll also hear from Zim, who thinks it's sad that other kids get to live with and know their birth parents but he doesn't. Sometimes Zim feels upset that he was adopted, but he doesn't really understand why he feels this way. How does he tell people that he was adopted? What if someone makes fun of him?

All these kids are amazing and have awesome stories to tell. So do you. We hope you recognize the things that make you amazing and special. We want you to see God's plan for your life and how your adoption experience can help others see how much God loves them, too.

We want you to know that you aren't alone—and you never were. The Lord has always been with you, even during your worst times. God brought you out of those bad places, and if you have accepted His love, He has adopted you into His family, just like your parents did.

The Bible says that God is a father to orphans and gives lonely people families (see Psalm 68:5-6). Even before you were born, God loved you. And if you trust in Jesus, you can be sure that God chose to adopt you as one of His own children (see Ephesians 1:4-5). You belong to your forever family, and you belong to Him.

By the end of this book, our prayer is that you will thank God for creating adoption and creating you. We also pray that you'll be ready and excited to share your story with others about what God has done in your life. Look for our later chapter about what a testimony is and how you can share your testimony with others!

In the book of Matthew, Jesus said,

"You're here to be light, bringing out the
God-colors in the world. God is not a secret
to be kept. We're going public with this,
as public as a city on a hill. If I make you
light-bearers, you don't think I'm going
to hide you under a bucket, do you?
I'm putting you on a light stand. Now
that I've put you there on a hilltop, on a
light stand—shine! Keep open house; be
generous with your lives. By opening up
to others, you'll prompt people to open up
with God, this generous Father in heaven."
MATTHEW 5:14-16, MSG

You can shine your light for others.

Our Story

Reid

Hi, my name is Reid. I was adopted as soon
as I was born, so I don't really know what it's
like not to be adopted. I was adopted because
my birth parents were never married. My birth

mother is from South Carolina, but my birth father is from Mexico and was living in the United States only for a little while. Patty and Miguel knew that making a plan for my adoption was better than having me live with just one of them. I'm glad I got to see Miguel a few times before he went back to Mexico, and I still get to visit with Patty a lot. I'm glad I was adopted, but sometimes I still wonder what it would be like if I wasn't.

I wanted to help write this book with my mother and my sister to tell kids that adoption isn't a bad thing. It's all part of God's amazing plan!

Halley

Hi, I'm Halley, Reid's younger sister. My birth mom, Suzie, was seventeen when she had me. She wasn't married and was still in school. She knew it would be hard to raise me, so she made an adoption plan. I've met Suzie, but I've never met my birth dad. Sometimes I wonder what it would be like if I wasn't adopted. I wonder if the times kids have made fun of me wouldn't have happened. But I like being adopted because

I can feel special, and I love my mom, dad, brothers, and our family dog very much.

I wanted to help write this book because I want kids who were adopted to know they're special and different in a good way. Hopefully, kids who were adopted will also give this book to their friends or anyone who has any questions about adoption.

Carey

Hi, I'm Carey. I'm the proud mom of Reid, Halley, and their younger brother, Benjamin. Reid, Halley, and Ben don't look anything like their dad (Kurt) or me. I often forget that these wonderful kids didn't come from my body, but as a family, we also realize that when the outside world looks at us, here's what they see:

- Dad: brown hair, blue eyes, white skin
- Mom: blonde hair, green eyes, white skin
- Reid: black hair, dark eyes, light-brown skin
- Halley: light-brown hair, hazel eyes, white skin
- Ben: brown hair, brown eyes, dark-brown skin

Even though we look different on the outside, on the inside we're a regular family. We love as a family; we disagree as a family; we behave as a family. We have a lot of the same likes, dislikes, character traits, and habits— both good and bad!

Reid, Halley, and I decided to write this book together because we couldn't find one like it already. Reid and Halley had some questions and thought they probably weren't the only ones who had them. So this book is for you and for anyone else who was adopted and has some questions. This book is also for family members and friends who *weren't* adopted— the people you think might like to know a little more about what makes your story so special.

Our Family

My husband, Kurt, and I wanted to be parents very, very badly. We got married and then started trying to have a baby biologically. Many months later I still wasn't pregnant, so Kurt and I went to the doctor, who told us we wouldn't be able to have a baby. This news made us sad. We were confused because we thought God wanted us to become parents, and we didn't know anything about adoption yet. But once we started learning about adoption, we thought it was an awesome way to have a family.

We followed the steps for adopting a child, and it took a while before we got a phone call. Finally our friend at the adoption agency told us, "There's a woman here who would like to meet you. She's going to have a little boy soon, and she wants you to be his mom and dad."

That baby boy was Reid. Kurt and I later adopted a girl, Halley, and another boy named Benjamin. We got to know Benjamin's birth mother and his biological half brother, Anthony. The boys' birth mother struggled with drugs when Ben was three years old, and Anthony came to live with us as a temporary foster care placement. After close to a year, their mother got better, and he was able to live with her again.

That's how foster care is supposed to work. Foster families care for children while their parents or caregivers get the help they need to take care of their kids the right way. The goal of foster care is to eventually return children to their families. But sometimes it doesn't work out that way, and the courts make the decision to give these kids the chance to be adopted by a forever family.

Kurt and I knew adoption would be a life-changing experience, even though it wouldn't always be easy. But we never could have guessed how truly incredible it is. We know that adoption has its challenges. In our situation, we still get to see Reid's, Halley's, and Ben's birth mothers. In some ways, it's like we're all part of a big family who loves each other very much.

We thank the Lord for creating adoption!

CHAPTER 1

WHY DID GOD CREATE ADOPTION?

FROM THE BEGINNING OF THE WORLD, GOD MADE MOMS AND DADS.

In the Bible, the book of Genesis describes how God created Adam and Eve to be together. (In Genesis 2:18, God said, "It is not good for the man to be alone.") Right after God made their bodies, He gave Adam and Eve the freedom to make their own decisions—good and bad. You might already know how those choices turned out, but if not, go to the Bible and start reading from the beginning!

One day Satan tricked Eve, and both she and Adam ate the fruit that God had told them not to. And that's when sin entered the world. We've all been making good and bad choices ever since. But the good news is that God created Adam and Eve as the first dad and mom! Even though they'd sinned, God loved them so much that He allowed them to live together as husband and wife.

This is God's perfect plan for families: A man and a woman get married first and then become parents.

But because the world we live in is no longer perfect, some couples are never able to physically create babies. Other couples have children before they're ready to be parents. And others want to be parents but aren't able to take care of their children for different reasons.

THE WORLD WE LIVE IN IS NO LONGER PERFECT.

JOHN:

"My birth dad was doing drugs and was hitting my birth mom and hurting her, and then he would hurt me. It wasn't too good. Whenever my birth parents didn't want me around, I would go to my grandparents' house. One day some person picked me up from their house and drove me away. I didn't know what was happening because I was only four years old, but I remember being hurt and scared. Then I found out I was being adopted.

"It turns out that my new sister had seen something about foster kids on TV and had really wanted brothers and sisters. So my mom decided to adopt my older sister and then found me later. I'm so happy that I live with my new family now. I think my adoption is all part of God's plan—I'm just not sure what His plan is yet."

Adoption is a subject that some very smart people have studied for a long time. We know that it helps in a lot of different ways. Adoption can help protect kids like John from sad and even dangerous living situations. It can help create new families where children get the care they need. Adoption also shows the world how great it is to be adopted into God's family. Remember how the Bible says that we as Christians are all adopted into God's family (Ephesians 1:5)? Your life is a picture of what God wants to do for each and every person in the world: He wants to rescue us and adopt us as His sons and daughters!

God is much smarter than all of us, and He works things together for the good of those who love Him (see Romans 8:28). And did you know there are stories in the Bible about adoption? Lots of people in the Bible were adopted. Let's read about some of them.

Moses (Exodus 1–2)

Moses was born during a time when baby boys were being killed. The king of Egypt—also known as Pharaoh—was worried that the number of Israelites was growing too rapidly. Pharaoh was afraid they would take over, so he told the women who helped deliver the Israelite babies to kill every newborn baby who was a boy. That's why, when Moses' mom and dad had a baby boy, they hid him for three months. I'm sure that was very difficult. But what happened next was even harder for Moses' parents: His mom made a floating basket, placed Moses in it, and then put him in the Nile river. She had no idea what was going to happen to Moses, but she trusted that God would take care of her son. And God did!

Guess who spotted that baby floating in the river? The daughter of Pharaoh, the very king who hated the Israelites! Pharaoh's daughter *adopted* the baby, and Moses grew up in the king's house. After he grew up, Moses went on to lead the Israelites to freedom—away from the evil king of Egypt. Moses would never have had the chance to save all those people if his parents hadn't trusted God and given their son a chance to be adopted.

Esther (Esther 2–7)

Esther was a beautiful young woman who was also an orphan. Esther's parents died when she was young, and her cousin Mordecai *adopted* her. One day Esther was taken to the royal palace, and the king of Persia married her. This made Esther the queen! But then an evil man who worked for the king decided he didn't like Jewish people and convinced the king to kill them all. What did that have to do with Esther? Well, she was also Jewish, but the king didn't know! So Mordecai and Esther came up with a plan to expose the evil man's plan. Esther convinced the king not to kill the Jewish people and saved the day. The Bible indicates that Esther had been placed in her role as queen "for such a time as this" (Esther 4:14, ESV). And it all started with Mordecai adopting Esther.

Jesus (Matthew 1:18-25)

The Bible tells us that Mary and Joseph were Jesus' parents when He was on earth. But

Joseph wasn't Jesus' birth father, was he? God placed Jesus in Mary's belly. Then when Jesus was born, Joseph basically *adopted* Him and raised Jesus as his own son. Did you ever think about how much you have in common with Jesus when He walked on the earth?

QUESTIONS TO THINK ABOUT

1. Why do you think God created adoption?

2. Who else in the Bible can you think of who was adopted and did something special?

3. How has reading these stories changed any of your feelings about being adopted?

CHAPTER 2

WHAT DOES THE BIBLE SAY ABOUT ADOPTION?

"Lots of awesome people in the Bible were adopted!"

The Bible has lots of verses about God's children being adopted into His family.

John 1:12 says, "Some people did accept [Jesus] and did believe in his name. He gave them the right to become children of God." When you ask Jesus to live in your heart, at that very moment you are adopted into God's family.

Does that mean God didn't love you before that moment? No way! God loves you so much that He sent His Son, Jesus, to die for your sins. He loves all of us so much that He lets us choose whether we want to be in His family. As soon as you pray, *Yes, Jesus, thank You for dying for me and saving me. Please come into my heart and be with me forever*, you're adopted. If you receive God's gift of love to you, then you are part of His family!

The Lord has plenty to say about adoption and caring for children without families. You can look it up for yourself and see how many times the Bible talks about these things. Here are some verses you can read:

- "My father and mother may desert me, but the LORD will accept me" (Psalm 27:10).
- "God is in his holy temple. He is a father to children whose fathers have died. He takes care of women whose husbands have died. God gives lonely people a family" (Psalm 68:5-6).
- "The LORD watches over the outsiders who live in our land. He takes good care of children whose fathers have died" (Psalm 146:9).
- "'Anyone who welcomes a little child like this one in my name welcomes me'" (Matthew 18:5).
- "'I will not leave you like children who don't have parents. I will come to you'" (John 14:18).

- "God sent his Son. A woman gave birth to him. He was born under the authority of the law. He came to set free those who were under the authority of the law. He wanted us to be adopted as children with all the rights children have" (Galatians 4:4-5).
- "God chose us to belong to Christ before the world was created. He chose us to be holy and without blame in his eyes. He loved us. So he decided long ago to adopt us. He adopted us as his children with all the rights children have. He did it because of what Jesus Christ has done" (Ephesians 1:4-5).
- "Here are the beliefs and way of life that God our Father accepts as pure and without fault. When widows are in trouble, take care of them. Do the same for children who have no parents" (James 1:27).
- "See what amazing love the Father has given us! Because of it, we are called children of God" (1 John 3:1).

Those are just a few of the times that the Bible mentions caring for children without families of their own. Adoption must be pretty important to God!

QUESTIONS TO THINK ABOUT

1. What does it mean to be adopted into God's family?

2. Have you prayed and asked God to adopt you into His family?

3. How does it feel to be God's child?

4. What is one of your favorite verses about adoption?

CHAPTER 3

WHY WAS I ADOPTED FROM FOSTER CARE?

ABBY:

"My birth parents were doing drugs and drinking alcohol and went to prison. When I was six, some adults ended up calling some social workers. I thought I was just going to spend the night at someone's house—they were taking all my stuff and putting it into trash bags. I went with a family from my church and stayed for six months, and then I went to another family, who adopted my sisters but not me. Then I went to another house for two months, then another for a year, then another. Now I've been with this family for six months, and they just adopted me last month!"

Did you know the foster care system goes all the way back to the 1800s? A New York City minister in the 1850s noticed a bunch of homeless and neglected kids living on the city streets, and he tried to find them families to live with. He actually put the kids on trains to different parts of the country so they could live with families who wanted to take care of them. Historians say this effort was the start of foster care in the United States.

Foster care has changed a lot since then, but it's still all about trying to find good homes for children who don't have them. Finding a good home for you didn't happen overnight, did it? While you were living in a tough situation, things were going on that you might not have known about.

First, someone probably noticed that you weren't being cared for properly. This could have been a family member, a teacher, or even a friend. That person cared about you so much that they contacted a government agency called child protective services. This agency is set up to make sure that every kid has food, clothing, a place to sleep, and someone who takes good care of them.

Second, when the people who work for this agency learn that children aren't safe or properly cared for, they take a look at what's going on in the home. Someone from the agency, usually a social worker, likely came to check on you. When the social worker saw what was happening, they decided to take you to a safe and healthy living situation.

As we already discussed, the main purpose of the foster care system is to help keep birth families together. Social workers do everything they can to help one or both birth parents get healthy enough to take care of their children the way they deserve. This might include getting medical treatment so the parents can stop using drugs or drinking alcohol. Or they may have to take parenting classes or see a counselor to learn how to handle their anger and not hurt their kids anymore. Parents also need steady jobs that will provide enough money for food and somewhere safe for their children to sleep. They have to meet with a social worker and even with a judge in court to get the help they need to address the issues in their family.

All this takes a lot of time. Sometimes it

works, and sometimes it doesn't. Some kids' parents know they're not doing a good job and are happy to get the help they need. But some parents give up because it's too hard.

ANTHONY'S STORY

Anthony's fifth-grade teacher noticed that he was missing school a lot. And when Anthony was in class, he wore the same clothes all the time and didn't have money for lunch. Then his birth mother got arrested for drugs. A social worker brought Anthony to live with our family because we had adopted his younger brother, Benjamin. After almost a year of living with us, Anthony went to live with his mother again. His mom stopped using drugs and got a lot of help learning how to take care of Anthony and herself. She also found a place to live and a job to support them.

When Anthony came to live with us, we had what's called a *kinship placement*. *Kinship* is an older word for a family relationship, so a kinship placement is when the social workers look for a good home that includes a family connection. Since Benjamin and Anthony were half brothers (they both have the same mother), the social workers asked if we could be Anthony's foster parents while his mother got better.

There are other places you might have lived during this time if a kinship placement wasn't available for you. There are group homes where many different kids live together. Or maybe you lived with a family you'd never met before. This is usually the case with a foster home.

Foster parents have to take a bunch of classes and be interviewed for a long time to make sure they can provide a good place for kids who are hurting to live for a while. Your foster parents also worked with your birth family to see if you could be reunited. Foster parents often take kids to family visits, court dates, and meetings with social workers.

Some children have better experiences than others in foster care. Hopefully you had a good relationship with your foster family, but if you had a bad time, we want you to know that we're sorry. And we're happy you don't have to go through that anymore.

While you were in foster care, the people who would later adopt you were getting ready to be your mom and dad. Do you know why they chose to adopt you? One big reason is that God spoke to their hearts. They felt that something—or someone—was missing from their lives. And that someone was you!

Or maybe your future parents learned about all the children in the foster care system who need safe and loving homes. Maybe they felt that God wanted them to open their home to one or more of these children. God wants us to care for children, and a great way to do that is by giving them a forever family to live with.

Of course, some moms and dads aren't able to biologically make a child, or sometimes they choose not to. And some parents choose to have both biological children *and* adopted children. No matter what each family's situation is, it definitely takes a lot of time and hard work to be a good parent.

So while you might have been going through some difficult times, your future parents were praying, praying, praying for you and doing the hard work necessary to bring you home. They had to fill out a lot of paperwork and go to classes and be interviewed a bunch of times in order to adopt you.

Maybe this was your situation, and your birth family couldn't work out the issues that had made child protective services pay attention. So the court terminated, or ended, your birth parents' parental rights. The court decided that you were going to be healthier, happier, and more secure in a different home than the one your birth parents could give you.

Adoption through foster care is just one way for kids in foster care to find their forever parents. Another way is that some children continue living with a foster family while they get to know their forever family. This helps everyone make sure that it's the best family situation for all of them.

ZIM:

"My birth mom couldn't take care of me. Some-times she hurt me when she got mad. I still wish she could've taken better care of me before I came to live with my mom and dad."

Zim was removed from his birth mother's home and entered the foster care system. When the court terminated the parental rights of Zim's birth mother, his foster family realized that God wanted Zim to be part of their family forever, and they adopted him.

Once you and your forever family found each other, did you go to court and tell a judge that you were all a new family? Did you get a new last name, or even a new first name?

Do you know what led to your placement in the foster care system? If you don't know much about your life before you were adopted, you might want to talk about it with your parents sometime.

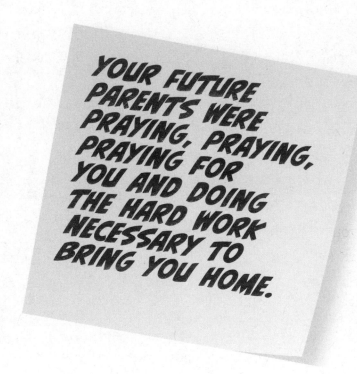

YOUR FUTURE PARENTS WERE PRAYING, PRAYING, PRAYING FOR YOU AND DOING THE HARD WORK NECESSARY TO BRING YOU HOME.

QUESTIONS TO THINK ABOUT

1. What have you learned from your parents about why they chose to adopt you?

2. What questions would you like to ask your parents about your adoption?

3. Do you remember how you felt when your foster parents told you they were adopting you? Can you describe what it was like?

4. If you could, what would you change about the foster care system or the adoption process?

CHAPTER 4

COULD I EVER BE GIVEN AWAY?

REID:

"When I was younger, a few times I thought my parents didn't love me when I got in trouble, and I wondered if they were going to give me away.

I didn't tell my parents I thought that for a long time—but when I finally did, they told me that would never happen. I felt so much better!"

If you lived in different foster homes before you were adopted, or if you were older when you got adopted, you might get scared. You might worry that your parents might not love you or will change their minds.

But once the adoption process is final, you belong to your parents, and they belong to you. At this point, there is no difference between a biological child and a child who's been adopted.

Whether you were adopted as a newborn, a toddler, or an older kid, your parents signed a bunch of papers, and then a judge signed and stamped them. These papers show that the government of the United States of America says that your adoptive parents are your legal parents and you are their legal child. What's even cooler is that your birth certificate now lists your adoptive parents as your mom and dad.

A birth certificate is a piece of paper everyone has that shows where and when they were born, what their name is, and who their parents are. So, no matter what anyone tells you, the people listed on your birth certificate are your mother and father, and the government of the United States agrees!

But sometimes it's hard to remember all that, especially when things go wrong at home.

When you break rules or get in trouble, you might worry that your parents won't love you as much anymore, or even that they might give you away. Well, guess what? Other kids feel this way, too, sometimes—even kids who weren't adopted. But the truth is that moms and dads don't like punishing their children. It's no fun at all, but your parents do it because they love you. Maybe that seems weird to you. Why would someone punish you and take away your stuff or the things you like to do, especially when you've already gone through some hard times?

Your parents discipline you because they're trying to teach you to do what's right. They hope that the more you learn to do what's right, the more you'll do it automatically. Keep in mind that the older you get, the more choices you'll face and the harder it can be to make the right decisions. Discipline trains you to obey your parents and make good choices.

Training your heart and mind is a lot like training your muscles. Athletes train their muscles in order to get stronger and better when they compete. Parents help children train their hearts and minds so they'll make wiser and better decisions. Your parents' job is to make your heart and mind so strong that by the time you grow up and leave home, you'll be able to make the right choices all by yourself.

Here's an example: Have you ever seen a two-year-old get mad and hit someone? Hopefully the mommy or daddy stopped their child and explained that hitting is wrong. But what if they didn't? Will this kid keep getting mad and hitting people at eight or ten or even twenty-five years old?

Do you think that parents are showing more love or less love by telling their two-year-old that it's not nice to hit others? Even if a punishment makes their children cry, moms and dads show love by teaching their kids to make good choices now. That way, as their children grow, they'll learn what is right and make better choices.

The Bible has a few things to say about parents helping their kids make good choices:

- "The LORD trains those he loves. He is like a father who trains the son he is pleased with" (Proverbs 3:12).
- "Train up a child in the way he should go" (Proverbs 22:6, ESV).

- "For the moment all discipline seems painful rather than pleasant, but later it yields the peaceful fruit of righteousness to those who have been trained by it" (Hebrews 12:11, ESV).

Of course, parents aren't perfect. Sometimes they make mistakes or get angry for the wrong reason. When parents get angry, it can bring bad thoughts to your mind too. But hopefully your parents apologize when they mess up.

Did you know that apologizing is a way of showing people how much you love them? Saying that you're sorry means you care about their feelings and want them to forgive you because you love them. (Some people have a hard time apologizing, but it doesn't mean they don't love you!)

So when you're in bed at night and bad thoughts come into your mind, remember how tricky Satan is. He will trick you into thinking that your parents don't really love you because you weren't born into your adoptive family.

Satan also tricks us by convincing us that it would be easier to lie than to tell the truth. He tempts us to think that it would be better to be selfish than to be generous with our brothers or sisters. He persuades us to believe that it would be more fun to disobey our parents or teachers than to obey them.

Satan plays these tricks on us to make us sin. Hopefully you're old enough to know that Satan is a big liar. Thoughts about your parents giving you away or not loving you are really just tricks that Satan is trying to play on you.

Did you know that you can make Satan get lost? You can say to yourself, *I'm not going to fall for those lies! I know that Jesus loves me, and so do my mom and dad!* The Bible says that if you stand up to the devil, "he will flee from you" (James 4:7, ESV). Just imagine Satan running away because you won't listen to him!

QUESTIONS TO THINK ABOUT

1. Have you ever worried that your parents might give you away? (If you have, you should definitely talk to them about your fears!)

2. Have you seen your birth certificate since you were adopted? What does it say?

3. Have you ever noticed Satan trying to trick you into feeling upset? How did you respond to his lies?

CHAPTER 5

WERE ANY FAMOUS PEOPLE ADOPTED?

REID:

"These people are amazing. They all did awesome things that changed the world and made it a better place."

Thousands and thousands of adoptions take place in the United States every year, and lots of them are adoptions from foster care. Children who were adopted have grown up to make amazing contributions to science, technology, entertainment, and sports. Many of them have also worked to promote the cause of adoption.

HALLEY:

"I think these people were able to make such big changes to the world because they were adopted. God placed them in special situations that allowed them to grow and have a chance to be great. And He can do the same for you!"

Here are just a few famous people who were adopted.

Steve Jobs: When Steve was born, his birth mother and birth father, who weren't married, chose adoption for him. They found Paul and Clara Jobs to care for Steve and be his parents. Paul and Clara lived in the Silicon Valley area of Northern California, where lots of cool computer stuff is made. Steve's dad was a skilled mechanic and craftsman, and he taught Steve how to design, build, and fix things. A few years later, Steve helped start the company that we know as Apple Inc. Do you or your parents have an iPhone, a Mac computer, or even Apple TV? You can thank Steve Jobs!

Faith Hill: Faith's birth mother wasn't married when she had Faith. She was visiting Mississippi when she placed Faith with her adoptive parents, Ted and Edna Perry. Faith's parents encouraged her to start singing in their church choir. One thing led to another, and now Faith is a very well-known country singer. Even cooler, she's married to another huge country superstar and actor, Tim McGraw, who was also adopted.

Jessica Long: Jessica was born in Russia and lived in an orphanage because she had a disability and had both of her lower legs amputated. An American couple adopted Jessica and encouraged her to start swimming when she was ten years old. She became the youngest member of the U.S. Paralympic Swimming team at the age of twelve and has won dozens of medals! Jessica says she owes everything she has to Jesus. "Since accepting Christ as my savior, I don't have to just go to God and have it all together," she said in a 2021 interview with MOVIEGUIDE. "He knows that I don't have it all together and I think it's something I still fight, that feeling of being in control and I am constantly reminded every day that I need to give it to God."

Dave Thomas: Have you ever eaten at a Wendy's restaurant? The founder of Wendy's was adopted as a baby and later created a charity to help find adoptive homes for children in the foster care system. As of 2021, the Dave Thomas Foundation for Adoption has found forever homes for more than ten thousand kids!

Aaron Judge: Aaron is an all-star baseball player for the New York Yankees. Aaron was the AmericanLeague Rookie of the Year in 2017, and in 2022 he broke the American League record for home runs in one season with sixty-two. Aaron was adopted by his parents when he was just two days old, but he didn't learn he was adopted until he was eleven. (His older brother, John, was also adopted.) At six foot seven, Aaron didn't get his height from his parents, but he says that he wouldn't be such a skilled baseball player if not for his adoptive parents, who taught him to work hard, to treat people kindly, and to love Jesus. Aaron frequently talks about his faith in God on social media.

Thanks to their adoptions, these people—and many others—were able to make big contributions to the world. God placed them in special situations that allowed them to help and inspire others.

Here are some other famous people who were either legally or unofficially adopted:

- **Eleanor Roosevelt** (the wife of President Franklin D. Roosevelt),
- **Edgar Allan Poe** (author),
- **Bill Clinton** (former president of the United States),

- **Nancy Reagan** (wife of President Ronald Reagan),
- **John Hancock** (one of America's founding fathers),
- **Simone Biles** (record-breaking Olympic gymnast),
- **Nelson Mandela** (former president of South Africa),
- **George Washington Carver** (inventor and scientist who made important changes in farming),
- **Leo Tolstoy** (author),
- **Colin Kaepernick** (professional football player), and
- **John Lennon** (founder of the famous music group the Beatles).

QUESTIONS TO THINK ABOUT

1. Can you think of some other well-known people who were adopted?

2. Who else do you know who was adopted, even if they aren't famous (yet)?

3. Do you think being adopted might help someone do incredible things? Why or why not?

CHAPTER 6

IS IT OKAY IF I GET MAD AT MY BIRTH PARENTS?

AVA:

"I was wandering the streets at about three years old, and the police found out I was getting hurt at home. I definitely don't care if I ever see my dad again. As for my mom, I'm just hoping she'll get better. When I get to feeling bad, I try to take a walk and think about finally having a family to go home to. I actually have someone I can have a relationship with and live with, and we're a family."

It's normal to feel upset about being adopted. You might also feel bad about what happened to you before and during your time in the foster care system. It's natural to be sad, frustrated, or confused. A lot of kids have these emotions at times, and it's not a bad thing for you to feel them. Let's talk about each of these feelings and how you can handle them when they rise up inside you.

Sad

It's very sad that your birth parents weren't able to care for you the way they needed to. If sin weren't part of our world, every single child would have a wonderful mother and father to live with. It's okay to feel sad that the world has sin in it and that your birth parents hurt you or couldn't protect you from the bad things that happened to you. It's also okay to be sad because you miss your birth parents sometimes. Your friends probably didn't experience the same tough times you did, and that can make you feel different from them. You might feel sad about that, too. Nobody likes to feel different or alone.

Frustrated

Frustration can rise up inside when you feel like you can't control a situation. As a kid, you might feel frustrated a lot. This can happen when you think your parents are bossing you around too much or because you have to go to school. Or you might feel frustrated because you can't go wherever you want or spend money the way you want to. Being frustrated about your adoption is normal too. You didn't have control over being taken out of your birth family's home and placed in foster care. You didn't have a choice about the foster family you lived with, or maybe even the family who adopted you. It's easy to feel frustrated about many things.

ZIM:

"Sometimes I'm glad I was adopted and sometimes I'm not. I get mad sometimes because other kids get to know their biological parents but my birth mom hurt me and others had to care for me."

Confused

Are you upset with your birth family *and* with the family who adopted you? Do you feel bad because they took you away from your birth family? Are you angry with your birth parents for allowing bad things to happen to you *and* angry when anyone says anything bad about them? Do you feel like you can trust your parents most of the time but also can't trust them sometimes? Do you ever feel guilty or upset because you still love and miss your birth mother or birth father?

It's confusing to feel these different ways, isn't it? These feelings are called mixed emotions, which is when you have what feel like opposite emotions at the same time. The good news is that these feelings are completely normal.

Adoption is tricky. It's an experience that can be happy and sad, easy and hard, normal and weird—all at the same time. It's sometimes confusing to think that God allowed something bad to happen so that something good could happen.

Mad

It's not fair, is it? Most of your friends probably live with one or both of their birth parents and have had safe, ordinary lives so far, right? It's okay to be angry that your birth parents had you but then may not have done a good job taking care of you.

If your birth parents or a previous family hurt you, you might have some confusing feelings about how to handle anger. We're so sorry that the people who were supposed to care for you and protect you made some poor choices. But we're happy that you're in a better place now.

Did you know that anger can be healthy? Anger is okay sometimes, as long as you use it the way God wants you to. We all have to learn to express our anger in healthy ways—not by hitting others or throwing things or hurting ourselves or other people. Anger can push us to deal with things we've been avoiding or even motivate us to help others who aren't treated fairly. In Ephesians 4:26, the Bible tells us to "be angry and do not sin" (ESV).

In other words, you need to make sure you express your anger the way God wants you to.

So when you're feeling sad, frustrated, confused, or mad, what should you do?

1. First of all, take a big, deep breath. We know grown-ups suggest this a lot, but it's really good advice. It's something that even adults need to do. Pausing to take a deep breath gives your body a chance to calm down so you can focus on how to start feeling better.

2. Talk to your mom and dad. They've seen a lot in their lives, so they can help you with your emotions. You can be honest with them about what you're feeling, and they will do their best to understand. So tell them when you start having these feelings. And if you're feeling these emotions a lot, your parents may want you to talk to another grown-up, such as a counselor. Counselors are awesome! They are like

doctors for your mind and emotions. They listen to you and help you understand what you're feeling so that you can feel better. There's nothing wrong with talking to a counselor. Both kids *and* adults should talk to someone when their feelings get so strong that they're hard to deal with.

3. Pray and read the Bible. There are many verses in the Bible that can help you with your emotions. Here are a few Scriptures to read:

- Proverbs 3:5-6: "Trust in the LORD with all your heart. Do not depend on your own understanding. In all your ways obey him. Then he will make your paths smooth and straight." Trust in God even when you don't understand. You might not understand, but He always does!

- Isaiah 41:10: "'Do not be afraid. I am with you. Do not be terrified. I am

your God. I will make you strong and
help you. I will hold you safe in my
hands. I always do what is right.'"
God is always with you, and He
promises to always help you.

- Jeremiah 29:11: "'I know the plans I
  have for you,' announces the LORD.
  'I want you to enjoy success. I do not
  plan to harm you. I will give you
  hope for the years to come.'" God's
  got this! He has a plan for your
  life.

- John 16:33 (MSG): "'You will be
  unshakable and assured, deeply at
  peace. In this godless world you will
  continue to experience difficulties.
  But take heart! I've conquered the
  world.'" Everyone has problems, but
  you can have peace knowing that
  Jesus is bigger than your problems.
  And you can have courage knowing
  that He is stronger than your
  problems too!

4. Take action! What do you enjoy
doing that could help you feel better?
Do you like to write? Then journal
about how you're feeling or write a
story about what's on your mind. Do
you like art? Then draw a picture or
paint a painting. Do you like to run
or play soccer or swim? Exercising
makes our bodies strong and healthy,
but it's also good for our minds and
our hearts when we're feeling down
about something. Think about one
of your favorite activities (healthy
stuff, not just screens), then turn
those thoughts into action and
see if it helps.

Your emotions are probably different and
more intense compared to the feelings of
someone who wasn't adopted. That's okay.
In fact, it's normal. What's most important,
however, is what you do with those feelings. If
anger, sadness, or frustration is growing stronger inside you, the joy of your new life with
your forever family will likely become smaller

and smaller. Thinking through and talking about those difficult feelings might be hard at the moment. But the more you think and talk about them *now*, the more joy you'll have in the days to come. We promise.

QUESTIONS TO THINK ABOUT

1. Do you feel sad, frustrated, confused, or mad sometimes? Which emotions do you feel most often?

2. What can you do when you experience these feelings? (Hint: Think about the four steps we discussed in this chapter.)

3. What else could you do to feel better when you have these feelings?

CHAPTER 7

IS IT NORMAL TO FEEL WORRIED OR SCARED SOMETIMES?

TRENT:

"I was with my biological parents for the first four years of my life. During that time I experienced domestic violence, neglect, and abuse. Finally, my four siblings and I were removed from the household, and most of us got split up. Unfortunately, the abuse didn't get better for a long time. I was in four different homes where there were different types of abuse occurring. Then I went to a foster care match event and met my adoptive parents. I would love to say that as soon as I walked into this home that was supposed to be forever, all my walls came down, my trust increased, and my self-esteem was restored, but unfortunately, that wasn't the case. It's not that simple or easy."

It's normal and understandable for you to feel worried or even scared at times. You've likely been hurt in the past, and maybe some people broke the promises they made to you. You've probably felt alone and scared, and you've probably wondered why you didn't get an easy, happy life. We're so sorry that all this has happened to you. We also hope you don't blame yourself for things that weren't your fault.

Most of all, we want you to know that you are not alone. God sees and knows everything you've gone through. He knows everything you're thinking and feeling. And because your new parents prayed and waited and worked so hard to welcome you into your forever family, we know that they care about your thoughts and feelings too.

Everyone worries more about some things than others, so you should talk, talk, talk with your parents about what worries you most. In this chapter, we've included some questions about things you might be worrying about and some ideas to help you start feeling better.

Does it bother you that your birth family couldn't keep you and take care of you the way you deserve?

It's no fun to think about how your birth parents didn't or couldn't always take care of you properly.

Your forever family wants the very best for you, and your parents' most important job is to protect you. Your parents also feel bad that your birth family wasn't always able to care for you. Good parents hurt when their children hurt, so you can talk to them about your emotions, and you can lean on them to help you feel better.

Do you sometimes feel like you have no control over what happens to you?

Before you were adopted, adults removed you from your birth family and placed you in one or more foster homes. Because of this, you might feel like you have no control over your situation. (That can definitely be a scary feeling!) Maybe you're still angry at the foster families you lived with. Or you might be upset with the social workers who took you away from your birth family.

Could you talk with your parents about having a few things in your life that you can control? This might include feeding or walking the family pet. Or maybe you could get a fish or a small pet to keep in your room and take care of. (A new pet can also be a big responsibility, so don't get upset if your parents don't think you're ready for it.)

Perhaps your parents would let you decorate your bedroom the way you want to—or part of your room if you share it with a sibling. (But that doesn't mean you don't have to keep it clean or pick up your dirty clothes when your parents tell you to!) Maybe you get to choose what to wear to school the next day or what snack to eat when you get home. Or perhaps you can pick out a special activity—like sports, art, reading, or a favorite show—that you can have time for each day or on weekends.

If you've gone through times when you haven't had enough food to eat, you might feel like keeping some food hidden, just in case. Or you might think you need to eat everything you can so you don't end up hungry again. That shouldn't be a problem with your forever family, but you might feel better if you learn to help whoever does the cooking in your house. It's actually pretty fun to look through cookbooks together and pick out new meals to try. Maybe you can help your parents plan each meal for the week and post the plan on the refrigerator so that you know what to expect every night.

When we had a child in foster care living with us, we posted our daily meal plan on the refrigerator. We also posted meal times and activities we had scheduled each day. It reminded us that we were going to have great times together as a family!

Do you sometimes worry that if you do something wrong, your parents won't want you anymore?

We've found in our family that it's best to talk about proper behavior in advance so that everyone knows the rules and what happens if we break them. ("If you break the rules, this will be the result.") And we always try to figure out together what's going on inside our hearts when we do something wrong.

Sometimes you might disobey your family rules because you feel like your parents or siblings don't love you. Those feelings can make you feel scared or upset. But you should know that your family members *do* love you, even when it doesn't always feel that way.

It can help to remind yourself how much your family loves you. A good way to do this is by getting together as a family and making a list of the things you love the most about each other. Then you could go around in a circle, and each of you could share what you wrote about other members of your family. You might be surprised to learn what your family enjoys about you!

Sometimes it's helpful to imagine switching places with different family members. For example, you could pretend you're the mom or dad, and one or both of your parents could pretend to be you. Then together you could act out a feeling you're having or something you're worried about. Of course, it's usually easier to talk about things that bother us when we're only pretending and aren't already upset.

Remember that your forever family wants you to love them just as much as you want them to love you. Your mom and dad probably have times when they feel like they're letting you down or not being good enough parents. All your family members will mess up at times, but try your best to trust them. Don't try to catch them making mistakes. It's okay to be sad or disappointed, but it's not okay to hurt others with your words or actions.

Do you sometimes worry that you've missed out on a lot of your adoptive family's history? Do you feel at times like you're still an outsider?

If you feel like you've missed out on your adoptive family's history, perhaps you and your parents could think of some fun traditions you can start as a family. These traditions will create new memories you all will share. Remember that you have a lifetime of memories to make together starting now!

You might recall some traditions from your birth family or a foster family you lived with.

Perhaps you could teach those traditions to your family now so they can enjoy them with you!

Before you came along, your family was missing a piece of the puzzle that made them complete. You don't enjoy looking at a half-finished puzzle as much as a completed one, right? So while your forever family does have

TRENT:

"I went to live with my parents when I was eight, and my adoption was finalized when I was nine. It took several years for me to really trust and open up to my adoptive parents about what was going on. Once I opened up about my past, I was able to start my healing journey. My parents helped me walk through all of it while pointing me to Christ the entire time. I was able to go from all that pain and abuse to overcoming it."

memories from before you came, the best memories are the ones you'll make together in the days and years to come.

QUESTIONS TO THINK ABOUT

1. Besides the situations we discussed in this chapter, what other worries and fears do you have?

2. What are some ways you can plan ahead for when you feel worried or scared?

3. What other ideas can you think of for making new memories with your forever family?

CHAPTER 8

WHAT IF PEOPLE MAKE FUN OF ME FOR BEING ADOPTED?

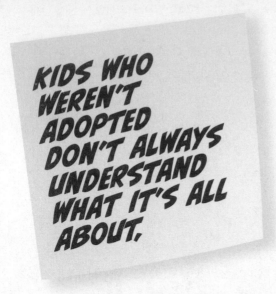

KIDS WHO WEREN'T ADOPTED DON'T ALWAYS UNDERSTAND WHAT IT'S ALL ABOUT,

and they sometimes make fun of kids who were adopted. Even your best friends might not really understand.

Your story is yours alone, and your family is different from other families. Your friends and their families don't know everything about your family, just like you don't know everything about them. Whether to share your adoption story with others is a choice that *you* get to make, especially as you learn which people you can trust with your story.

When you're with your parents, think about which people you'd feel safe sharing your story with and what you might say to them. Your mom and dad can help you decide what's okay to talk about with others and what things might be better for just your family to know. Our family has decided that we will tell only our close friends about our adoption stories. These are the people we love and trust the most.

We understand that even nice people can make poor choices. A bad choice might be something small, like eating too many treats instead of a healthy snack. Or it might cause hurt and tears—like others saying mean things when they find out you were adopted. This doesn't actually make them bad people; it just means they're making bad choices. Poor choices can also happen when people don't realize or understand that they're hurting you.

Think about that for a moment: If others don't realize that their words are hurtful, then it certainly won't do any good for you to get mad or try to hurt them back. It's better to tell someone that they hurt your feelings first— before you get angry and maybe make a bad choice yourself!

ABBY:

"All I can say is that if someone's making fun of you, they don't understand what it's like to be adopted from foster care. I honestly think that being adopted is more special because you've gone through so much and have more people to love— a bigger family to love."

Here are some things you can do if someone makes fun of you or your adoption story:

- Ignore the person and simply walk away. You don't need to act angry or upset. Walking away just gives the person a minute to think about how mean it was to say those things.

- Calmly explain to the person that being adopted just means that you have extra people who chose you to be part of their family. Being adopted isn't bad; it's actually pretty great! Say that you're happy to answer any questions about adoption. But if the person is trying to hurt your feelings, explanations probably won't work. In that case, you might want to stay close to adults or trusted friends when the mean person is around.

- If the person won't stop making fun of you, consider telling a grown-up, such as a teacher or your parents.

- Don't ever believe someone who says that adoption is bad or something to be ashamed of! You already know that being adopted means that you're special and your family loves you very much. It *doesn't* mean you've done something wrong. Adoption simply means that God has a plan for your life that included adoption.

- Most important, try to forgive the person who teased you. This might be the hardest step to take when people make fun of you, especially if they don't understand how badly they hurt you or don't say they're sorry.

Forgiveness is important whenever someone hurts us. The Bible has a lot to say about forgiveness. First, it says we should forgive other people who hurt us because God has forgiven us time and time again. God is perfect and never messes up, yet He still forgives us when we mess up or don't obey Him.

The Bible also says that forgiving other people makes our lives better. It's hard to be happy when you're upset with someone. Not forgiving someone means holding on to that anger rather than letting it go. Unforgiveness keeps us from being the best and happiest we can be.

Forgiving someone who hurt you doesn't mean you have to pretend that it never happened. You might need to stay away from people who make fun of you, especially if they don't realize they are hurting your feelings. That's okay. It's sometimes better to stay away from someone for a time if you know it's not a good situation.

Forgiving people isn't just for them. We also forgive so that we can feel better. Forgiveness is like putting a bandage on a cut finger. It doesn't make the pain go away, but it protects the cut and helps it heal faster. Maybe when you're ready, you can even tell people that you forgive them for hurting your feelings. And that might lead to telling them that you forgive others because Jesus forgave you!

Here are some things the Bible has to say about forgiveness:

- """Forgive us our sins, just as we also have forgiven those who sin against us"""" (Matthew 6:12).
- "'Forgive other people when they sin against you. If you do, your Father who is in heaven will also forgive you. But if you do not forgive the sins of other people, your Father will not forgive your sins'" (Matthew 6:14-15).
- "Be kind and tender to one another. Forgive one another, just as God forgave you because of what Christ has done" (Ephesians 4:32).
- "Put up with one another. Forgive one another if you are holding something

against someone. Forgive, just as the Lord forgave you" (Colossians 3:13).

QUESTIONS TO THINK ABOUT

1. Has anyone ever made fun of you after they found out you were adopted? How did that make you feel?

2. If you have been teased or made fun of, what did you do?

3. What's the hardest thing about forgiving people who make fun of you? Can you pray right now and ask Jesus to help you forgive them?

CHAPTER 9

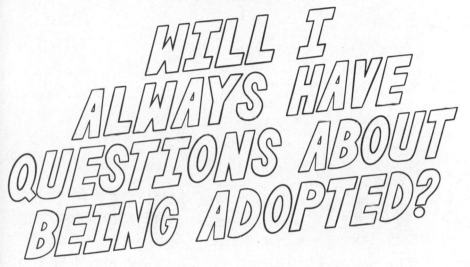

WILL I ALWAYS HAVE QUESTIONS ABOUT BEING ADOPTED?

ZIM:

"I was excited when I met Reid and Halley and found out that they were adopted too. We have that in common and can talk to each other about it."

Adoption and foster care sure are complicated, aren't they? And they often come with a lot of complicated feelings and questions. The way you felt about being adopted when you were little is probably different from how you feel about it now. You likely have questions today that you didn't have when you were younger. And when you turn fifteen or seventeen or twenty, you might have even more questions.

When you were a little kid, maybe three or four years old, you might have heard that you were adopted, but you probably didn't fully understand what that meant. As time passed, you likely started asking questions. That's what Reid and Halley did.

Maybe you've asked some of the questions we've talked about in this book or even had other questions:

- "Why didn't my birth parents take proper care of me?"
- "Was it my fault that I had to go into foster care?"
- "Will I ever have to go back to my birth family or to another foster home?"

Your parents probably tried to give you simple answers to these hard questions. That's because they knew back then that you couldn't understand the situation the way you can now. And your parents' answers might have been good enough for you at the time.

The older we get, however, the more we begin to understand more complicated things. When you become a teenager, you might have even more complex questions and feelings about adoption than you do now—especially about your own adoption. That's okay, and it's definitely normal! Feeling emotions and asking questions can lead to positive things.

People have changed human history by asking tough questions or feeling so strongly about the wrongs they've seen that they've decided to do something about it!

As you get older, you might want to know if you can contact or visit members of your birth family. (Or you might not, and that's okay too.) Talk to your parents about what you're hoping or feeling. Right now might not be the best time for a visit, but you might begin the process by writing letters to help express your feelings. You could include letters to brothers, sisters, grandparents, and even friends you knew from before you were adopted.

You probably won't want to mail your letters until you and your parents agree that the time is right. For now, just keep them safe somewhere, but start praying for your birth family. Pray that they will find Jesus if they don't know Him already. Prayer is like a superpower: The universe's most powerful superhero—Jesus—is on your side! He loves working wonders when we pray. So pray for your birth family and trust God to do what's best. If He wants you to have a relationship with them, He can make it happen. He's always got your back.

But remember . . . adoption is only part of your story!

Your adoption does make you different from others. But hopefully you realize that God made every single person different. Even though it can feel like the biggest deal in the world, being adopted is just one part of who you are. Always remember that. It's good to ask questions about being adopted and talk about your feelings when they come up. But don't let your feelings take charge of your life.

The Bible warns us about letting our thoughts and desires become too important in our minds and hearts (see Romans 12:2-3). If you spend your time thinking about being adopted or spending time in foster care, these thoughts can start to control your life. You might start wanting extra attention or special treatment because you were adopted or because difficult things happened to you.

You don't want these desires to control your mind. Your thoughts and questions about being adopted are important. But if they become too important, they'll push aside the blessings in your life—your family, your friends, your talents, even God. Then you won't be happy at all.

You are different and special, but not just because you were adopted. Everyone you know is different and special, even if they weren't adopted! Your friends are special because they're kind or smart or good at sports, or simply because they listen when you need someone to talk to.

It's normal and healthy to talk about your questions and feelings about being adopted. Just make sure you spend lots of time talking and thinking about *other* things that make you special and different. All these things make you *you*!

QUESTIONS TO THINK ABOUT

1. What questions do you still have about adoption?

2. Imagine yourself as a teenager or even a grown-up. How do you think your feelings about adoption might change when you're older?

3. Other than adoption, what makes you special and different from others?

CHAPTER 10

WHAT'S NEXT FOR ME?

TRENT:

"I'm twenty-one now and am trying to help others find that same healing I've been able to find. This journey is not easy, but now I can give others the hope I was able to receive and pay that forward to help them heal."

Have you ever heard the word *testimony*? This word is usually used in courts of law. In court, witnesses give their testimonies, which means they describe what happened or what they saw. But a Christian shares a different kind of testimony. When we give our testimonies as Christians, we might describe what God has done in our lives. Or we might share the story of how we came to ask Jesus to live in our hearts forever.

When we ask Jesus to come into our hearts, it's because we believe that He is real and that He loves us. There's always a story behind this decision, and everyone's testimony is different and special to them.

Adoption will always be part of your testimony. You can now see how Jesus was with you even before you were born. He was with you during your scariest and loneliest moments. He has always loved you, and He even made a way for you to be adopted into your forever family. You can use your adoption testimony to encourage other kids who have been adopted and have strong feelings about it. You can also use it to encourage adults to consider foster care and adoption. And you can use your adoption testimony to encourage others to ask Jesus to live in their hearts. That's pretty exciting!

We're so grateful that adoption is part of our forever family's testimony. First of all, we love each other so much and couldn't imagine not being together. Second of all, we get to use our family's testimony to tell others about adoption and how Jesus made our family even more awesome! We've talked with people in person about adoption and foster care, but now we get to use our testimony in this book to encourage you!

We've included space at the end of this chapter where you can write your adoption story—your testimony. Your adoption testimony might help kids like you right now. And when you grow up, it might help many other people who have been adopted.

As we near the end of this book, spend a few minutes talking to God. Pray that He will give you peace and comfort about being adopted. Also pray for wisdom and direction in using your adoption testimony to show how good God is. Ask Him to use your story to lead others to choose adoption and to know Jesus as their Savior.

Just like you prayed to ask Jesus to come live in your heart, you could pray something like this:

Dear God,
I might not understand all the reasons why
You chose adoption as the plan for my life,
but I love You and trust You. I know that
You have a purpose for me and my family
and that You wouldn't have chosen this life
for me if You weren't with me to help me

handle it. Thank You for rescuing me from my difficult times and for bringing me to a new family. Thank You that my forever family chose to adopt me. Please give me courage to share my testimony with others so they can come to know You better and maybe even think about adopting. Use my adoption story to show others how good You are.

I love You, Lord. Amen.

My Adoption Testimony

_____

_____

_____

_____

_____

_____

_____

_____

_____

_____

_____

_____

DO I BELONG?

Teach Your Friends the Language of Adoption

SAY THIS, NOT THAT

placed or chosen for adoption	*not*	given up or put up for adoption
birth mom or birth dad	*not*	real mom or real dad
was adopted	*not*	am adopted
multiracial family	*not*	mixed family
son or daughter	*not*	adopted son or adopted daughter
waiting child	*not*	adoptable child or unwanted child
birth or biological child	*not*	natural or real child

Adoption Words and Their Meanings

adoption from foster care. This happens after a court has terminated (ended) parental rights and approved your adoption. A new family is found—maybe your current foster family—who would like to adopt you. After a period of time, the court approves the papers stating that your new family is now your legal forever family.

closed adoption. This means that, for many different reasons, you won't see or speak with your birth family after your adoption. Some, but not all, adoptions are closed because the birth parents wanted it this way at the time.

domestic adoption. This means that you were born in the same country where your adoption took place.

finalized adoption. This means that your adoption is legal and final and that there is no difference between a biological child and a child who was adopted. You are a permanent member of the family who adopted you, and you share their last name. Your birth certificate says that the people who adopted you are your parents, and you won't be given back or sent away.

forever family. This is what your new permanent family is sometimes called, especially if you were adopted as an older child. This means that you are theirs and they are yours forever and ever!

foster care. This refers to your living situation if you're taken out of your birth family's home because you were left alone or not cared for properly. Foster care might involve living with another family or in a group home until you are either (1) reunited with your birth family or (2) adopted into a forever family.

international adoption. This means that you were born in a different country from the country where your parents live. They brought you to live with them.

open adoption. This means that even though you were adopted, you still have a relationship with your birth family. You might see each other once in a while, or you might just send pictures and letters.

reunification. This happens if you go back and live with your birth family.

termination of parental rights. This happens when a court of law determines that your birth family is unable or unwilling to care for you properly. The rights of your birth parents are terminated (ended), and the court decides that you should live with a family who can treat you well, keep you safe, love you, and raise you to be a good person. Sometimes this means that you will live with a foster family until your forever family adopts you.

FOCUS ON THE FAMILY®